The Witness of Your Wardrobe

D0166539

The Witness of Your Wardrobe

Bible Principles for Today!

By

John and Donna Bishop

SWORD of the LORD PUBLISHERS

Post Office Box 1099 • Murfreesboro, Tennessee 37133

All Scripture quotations are from
the King James Bible.

Printed and Bound in the United States of America

Table of Contents

1
THE RIGHT APPROACH

Introduction

We have now come to a controversial topic in most Christian circles. It is the topic of dress. This covers a lot more than just clothes. We must deal with attitude and spirit as well as the Scriptures. Our clothes truly reflect our attitude and say a great deal about us. In this study I am going to use the Bible as our primary source of information, as it must be in everything we discuss.

This book has been in the works for years. I have researched earnestly for months to make sure that I present the facts as clearly as I can. I have searched the Internet and spent hundreds of dollars in purchasing both secular and biblical books on the history of dress. I have intentionally sought Christian authors that have different backgrounds and perspectives from mine so that I wouldn't have only one way of looking at the subject. And, yes, I have read those who would support some of the positions I hold. I have really grown spiritually while doing this study. I hope you will also.

In my research, I have been surprised and even shocked by how open and vocal secularists are about the subject of dress! I allowed my wife to filter pictures of women in my materials for me so that I wouldn't have unclean images in my mind. She had to throw away some of the materials, but she was able to clean up some of them enough so that I could use their thoughts for insight. I always try to practice the principles of purity of mind commanded to us in Philippians 4:8:

> *"Finally, brethren, whatsoever things are true, whatsoever things are honest, whatsoever things are just, whatsoever things are pure, whatsoever things are lovely, whatsoever things are of good report; if there be any virtue, and if there be any praise, think on these things."*

A clean mind and a clean heart feel so good! I never want to jeopardize that wonderful peace with something tainted.

Main Goals

I do not want to get so caught up in what I believe is important on the issue of dress that I lose sight of what my main goals are in writing this book in the first place. My main goals consist of the following:

1. Challenge the church to stand on the issues of modesty, purity and chastity in such a way that our dress and outward appearances reflect a Christlike spirit.

2. Reevaluate our present stand or viewpoint concerning dress and restudy some of the biblical passages that address the issue of outward adorning. Some passages of Scripture seem to me to be discarded or ignored for various reasons, and they need a new look and study for our day. In every age of Christendom there seem to be biblical issues that need to be revitalized or renewed for the benefit of the church and its influence on the world. It appears to me that dress is one such issue today!

3. Remind Christians how love, the most important Christian virtue of all, is vitally connected to the issue of dress. Loving the Lord, lost people and everyone around

us should motivate us to modify or at least review our tastes and choices. We must all be reminded that clothing sends a very loud message to those around us about who we are and even what we believe. Galatians 5:13 says:

"For, brethren, ye have been called unto liberty; only use not liberty for an occasion to the flesh, but by love serve one another."

4. Try to unite believers with different ideals and tastes in some way so that we can respond to our culture's influence on our Christian faith and uniqueness in this matter of dress. I fear we have been so influenced by the world around us that we are in grave danger of losing the distinctiveness of the Christian faith in general. When believers and leaders in the Christian faith say, "It does not matter how you dress," they are in danger of denying—not just ignoring—God's Word on the subject! We must rise up with a united voice and say, "Enough!"

Reasons for Writing

I chose to write this book because I wanted to include a lot of the thoughts that I didn't mention in the book I wrote in 1980. Maybe it's a sign of the times, or maybe I have grown more to understand how very important it is to have right motives. I want to use primarily the Bible, but also other sources to teach us how very important dress is, particularly for women.

I am going to all this work for several more reasons:

1. In working with teens and teaching these issues every week for at least the last twelve years, I have learned a few things about what does and doesn't work. I have noted not just how teens react at the camp, but I have gotten feedback from them after they have left camp and gone back to their churches. I am not implying that the Bible doesn't always work, but *how* we teach the Bible surely makes a lot of difference!

2. I believe that most ladies are sincere about this topic and want further information to make the right decisions. In other words, I believe the best instead of the worst about most ladies. I think they have been deceived and misled by the world. In fact, many have told me this after hearing me teach a lesson regarding this issue.

3. These times call for more information and encouragement simply because ladies nowadays do not have the examples from their mothers and grandmothers that I and others of my generation had.

My only memories of my mom are the few weeks that I had with her after my illness until she went Home to be with the Lord. In that time, she tried to tell me everything I needed to know. (I asked my family not to tell me everything about my life before losing my memory to meningitis, just the important things!) She said I led her to the Lord after I was saved at the age of fifteen. She had been enslaved to alcohol, as were my father and stepfather, whom I also led to the Lord before they died. However, she told me that even before she was saved she wouldn't wear a pair of pants to church because of her godly mother, my mama. She said that when Mama worked in the fields, she would wear a long dress that dragged on the ground over her pants. Mama was concerned about both modesty and femininity.

Don't turn me off simply because I said the word *pants* right here. We will discuss that hot topic a little later. Keep the main focus on modesty right now. Yes, Mama was an old-fashioned Baptist, not Amish or even Pentecostal. That was the way a lot of women dressed then. Sadly, many don't remember those days. So now we must help others who have grown up in an entirely different culture. They have grown up under a different set of rules, and they need to know some of the history of attire to appreciate where we came from and where we are headed.

4. I do not believe that all indecency in the church is intentional. Some of it is done ignorantly and even innocently. I have seen young girls who do not yet understand the dangers of lust dressing provocatively because somebody dressed them up that way! They have no idea why it is wrong! We need greater clarity and information to combat worldly influences such as Britney Spears. Many of us knew her innocent looks weren't real, and, before long, she showed the world that she wasn't innocent. The sad thing is that she took many young girls down the wrong road with her.

Love Should Be Our Priority

I think because this topic is so very touchy in this day, we all need to step back with a loving attitude and restudy and review the biblical principles involved in this heated debate. We have all been in danger of forgetting or neglecting some very important principles related to believers' dress simply because of the age in which we live. I do not think most Christians are as guilty of *rejecting* truth on this subject as they are of *forgetting* or *neglecting* truth. We all probably know some Christians who may be guilty of rejecting truth in favor of going along with the crowd, but many Christians simply have not heard a pastor or Bible teacher teach on this topic for years. I hear that all the time these days!

I am not calling on Christians to ignore our culture and turn to the dress of the Middle East or even the styles of the early 1940s. I am asking Christians to remember our heritage and return to purity, modesty and charity. Charity, or love, should guide our decisions and control our actions. We should have a love for God, His Word and the world of lost people He so much wants us to reach for Him.

"Let all your things be done with charity."—I Corinthians 16:14.

5

The Witness of Your Wardrobe

"Now the end of the commandment is charity out of a pure heart, and of a good conscience, and of faith unfeigned."—I Timothy 1:5.

"For, brethren, ye have been called unto liberty; only use not liberty for an occasion to the flesh, but by love serve one another"—Galatians 5:13.

The goal of all of God's guiding commandments and principles is love. If we fail to love, then we fail to be obedient to God even if we look the part!

Some may feel it would have been nice if God had spelled out every little detail on clothing. Since He knows the future as well as the present, He could have used terms like *culottes*, but God's silence demands that we know Him well enough that we seek His face for guidance. God is silent about several things, and I have thought, *It would sure make life easier if He had just listed them in one extra book.* But then I began learning that we need His silence to learn to live by love more than laws, and true love never does anything to hurt the Lover of our heart, soul and body.

We are designed for a divine relationship, not just divine rules. But a loving relationship does not resent rules from a loving Caregiver. For instance, God says in I John 5:3 that His commandments are not grievous to those in whom His love dwells. Love not only makes His commandments bearable but enjoyable. The difference is love! Does it really come across as loving to say, "I'll wear what I want, and it is nobody's business"? Where is the love when a girl says, "It's not my problem if a boy or a man lusts because of the way I am dressed. That is their problem"? Read this testimony from an honest young man:

As a guy in my twenties, when I see what girls are wearing and what the style is today, it makes it that much harder to stay pure in heart. I think many young women don't realize the signals they are send-

6

ing men with the way they dress.

I think it would be much more loving to say, "I do care what others think, and I want to make sure I do right." The choice is not rules *or* love; the true choice should be rules *with* or *without* love. Rules are inevitable, but we must choose to love along with the rules.

I will not do you the disservice of trying to give you a list of dos and don'ts. One of the most dangerous things I could commit would be to add to God's Word, even if it were out of a desire to be safe. That might be what the Pharisees did. Their sincere desire might have been to keep people from breaking God's true laws, so they made up over six hundred of their own which eventually became laws themselves. God forbid that I would do that!

Godliness Should Be the Focus

"For the grace of God that bringeth salvation hath appeared to all men, Teaching us that, denying ungodliness and worldly lusts, we should live soberly, righteously, and godly, in this present world."—Titus 2:11, 12.

"But refuse profane and old wives' fables, and exercise thyself rather unto godliness. For bodily exercise profiteth little: but godliness is profitable unto all things, having promise of the life that now is, and of that which is to come."—I Timothy 4:7, 8.

Our goal as Christians should be to become more like God. A godly testimony will surely affect how we act, including how we dress!

Right now I want to give you a really great principle taught to me by Dr. S. M. Davis. I have his permission to quote him on this topic of dress. I would encourage every reader to get his DVD series on this topic. (Information on how to purchase this is given at the end of the book.) He says that THE MOST IMPORTANT CLOTHING OF THE CHRISTIAN ISN'T OUTWARD CLOTHING BUT INWARD

The Witness of Your Wardrobe

CLOTHING! Read these wonderful Scriptures:

"Her clothing is silk and purple....Strength and honour are her clothing; and she shall rejoice in time to come."—Proverbs 31:22, 25.

"Put on therefore, as the elect of God, holy and beloved, bowels of mercies, kindness, humbleness of mind, meekness, longsuffering....And above all these things put on charity, which is the bond of perfectness."—Colossians 3:12, 14.

"I will greatly rejoice in the LORD, my soul shall be joyful in my God; for he hath clothed me with the garments of salvation, he hath covered me with the robe of righteousness."—Isaiah 61:10.

"Yea, all of you be subject one to another, and be clothed with humility: for God resisteth the proud, and giveth grace to the humble."—I Peter 5:5.

I believe there are some principles on which we can all agree. I want us to find them first. Then we will discuss the ones on which we probably don't all agree but which we need to consider and apply to our lives in some way or other.

We cannot just simply write off everything the Bible says about dress, nor can we simply say that it is all outdated material that does not apply to us in any way today. We must avoid the attitude widely held today that dress is just relevant to culture or that we can only have preferences. Some say there is no room for convictions in dress, just personal opinions or preferences. We cannot take this approach, it seems to me, without the possibility of doing an injustice to other Scriptures that we clearly and firmly apply today. Scriptures such as those related to smoking, gambling, etc., give us principles to which we hold tenaciously for our day but which are, in all honesty, not as clearly spoken as those on dress.

Nearly all believers think that the Ten Commandments

8

apply to people in our day and that the rejection of these eternal moral values has nearly destroyed our society. Are these the only lasting values and principles in the Old and New Testaments that apply to us today? Of course not! We are all in trouble if we take that approach, and I will seek to make that clearer later on.

A Request, Not a Requirement

Let me hasten to say some very important things just now. I want this whole book to reflect a humble and caring spirit. If in any way and at any time it comes across as harsh, rude or un-Christlike, then I have failed in my wording. Forgive me if my selection of words comes across in any way other than that of a preacher who cares for others and desires that we all see and follow God's precious principles in every area of our lives, including dress.

PLEASE REMEMBER THIS: I AM TRYING TO MAKE A PLEA MORE THAN I AM TRYING TO MAKE A POINT! THIS IS MORE OF A REQUEST THAN A REQUIREMENT THAT I AM MAKING!

Some of my remarks and conclusions will be regarded by some as extreme, outdated and really of little importance. Please realize something about me that is very important to keep in mind as you follow the thoughts behind my words: I am convinced we Christians are in a battle and struggle for our lives and existence! The battle with the world, the flesh and the Devil is very real to me.

The erosion of moral values, marriage and ethics has taken an awful toll on the church today. I sincerely believe that many Christians have surrendered an important weapon in this battle to the enemy of our souls, and that weapon is how we dress. This surrendered weapon is certainly not as important as other weapons, such as our Bible-based beliefs about the inspiration of God's Word and the issues of abortion, creationism and the winning of souls. Yet, this issue is important and is tied to all of the above in some sense or other. I hope you will see this.

Let's get started with this prayer: "Please, Lord, show me Your truth. I am willing to be shown truth that I may have rejected or neglected in the past. I truly love You and believe Your Word is truth! Amen!"

2
MODESTY

In discussing modesty, we will get nowhere with somebody that writes off the whole dress issue with words often used out of context in I Samuel 16:7:

> "For the LORD seeth not as man seeth; for man looketh on the outward appearance, but the LORD looketh on the heart."

It is very dangerous to take words from the Bible that do not pertain at all to a particular subject and use them to support a dogmatic stand on that subject. God's prophet wasn't talking at all about how David was dressed, but rather about his youthfulness, his experience or perhaps inexperience, as well as his physical size compared to his older brothers.

I have never in all my life heard a preacher, no matter how strong a stand he takes on dress codes, state that what is on the outside is more important than what is in the heart! Nobody in their right mind thinks that! But to casually suggest that "God isn't really concerned with what we wear," as one radio preacher stated after reading this passage, is truly wrong! God has clearly stated in several Scriptures that our dress is important! Certainly there are more important things, but if God takes time to say something about it, that makes it important! First Samuel

16:7 does not cancel out those Scriptures dealing with dress. As a matter of fact, the two main passages on dress that I call attention to later on both place great emphasis on the heart, attitude and spirit of the people taught to dress in His way.

Let there be no mistake about this: I BELIEVE THAT WHAT IS IN THE HEART IS MORE IMPORTANT THAN WHAT IS ON THE BODY, BUT WHAT IS IN THE HEART WILL EVENTUALLY AFFECT WHAT IS ON THE BODY!

We all know that God's clear call and command for godly women is to dress in "modest apparel." First Timothy 2:9 says,

> "In like manner also, that women adorn themselves in modest apparel, with shamefacedness and sobriety; not with broided hair, or gold, or pearls, or costly array."

That is a clear-cut command that simply cannot be ignored. But what does it mean?

Some Christians use Paul's teaching in I Timothy, chapter 2, to guide ladies to dress right or modestly in the Lord's house on the Lord's Day, but state that to some degree the rest of the week is left to each person's conscience. When you think of this in the light of the whole of Scripture, would it seem possible that God would make modesty a guideline just for the church building or meeting place and not for a testimony to the rest of the world? Of course we are not left in the dark as to the answer to that question. What is said here is not just for church meetings. God uses some of the exact same wording about modesty in I Peter, chapter 3, and He applies it to the home as well.

Modesty Defined

God does not always give us definitions of terms He uses in His Word. The word *modest* is not defined in the

Bible, because the Bible is not a dictionary. We learn the meaning of words by the context in which they are used, through dictionaries that contain definitions of the original biblical languages behind the English words, through old and new English dictionaries and through the definitions of great and noble Christians of today and days past. So let us get started. I will start with the biblical context and then use a tool called the *Strong's Concordance,* which defines the Greek and Hebrew words of the Scriptures.

To begin with, we can easily make some observations about I Timothy 2:9, the only place the English word *modest* is found in the King James Bible. (This is the translation I will use exclusively for this book.) It is obvious from the passage in I Timothy that modesty is in contrast to excessive hairdos and jewelry: "...not with broided hair, or gold, or pearls, or costly array."

Now let's see what is excessive by comparing Scripture with Scripture. God deals with the issue of women's dress in I Peter 3:3: "Whose adorning let it not be that outward adorning of plaiting the hair, and of wearing of gold, or of putting on of apparel." God is not saying that ladies should not wear apparel; therefore, we know that He does not mean that they should not wear jewelry or braid their hair. This passage simply means that women should not wear these items excessively to the point that they could possibly send a message other than godliness.

My wife is very careful about not overdoing her makeup or jewelry. She does not want to be excessive lest it hinder her from reaching others for Christ. Modesty does have something to do with culture, but it is more than that. You can do something that might be scripturally correct and yet immodest in another culture. Love must be our guiding principle where the Bible is silent on specific issues. How many rings are too many? How much makeup is too much? I can't tell you, but I

The Witness of Your Wardrobe

can tell you this: you must be careful to exercise moderation when choosing adornments.

Moderation should be the testimony of every Christian as the Lord's coming draws closer. Philippians 4:5 says, "Let your moderation be known unto all men. The Lord is at hand." Are you known for moderation? This word "moderation" is speaking primarily of our attitude or spirit. It is also translated in the King James Bible as *gentle* and *patient*. I love how the *International Standard Bible Encyclopaedia* attempts to bring together the great fullness of meaning for this word *moderation*.

Hastings prefers "considerateness" or "sweet reasonableness" (HDB, III, 413); "Gentleness" and "forbearance" are too passive. The "considerateness" of the Bible, whether applied to God or man, is an active virtue. It is the Spirit of the Messiah Himself, who will not break the bruised reed nor quench the smoking flax, and it is the spirit of every follower who realizes that "the Lord is at hand." The want of this "considerateness" too often mars our religious life and spoils its influence.

Oh, may God give us all a "sweet reasonableness"!

Now let's explore some definitions of *modest* found in English dictionaries.

1. arising from or characteristic of a modest nature
2. observing the proprieties of dress and behavior
3. decent: limited in size, amount, or scope (as in, a family of *modest* means)
4. unpretentious (as in, a *modest* home)

Synonyms are *shy* and *chaste*.
Merriam-Webster Online

1. humble: unwilling to draw attention to your own achievements or abilites
2. shy: not confident or assertive, and tending to be easily embarrassed

3. reasonable: not large, extreme, or excessive (as in, a modest income)
4. simple: not showy, elaborate, or pretentious (as in, a modest dwelling)
5. not overtly sexual: reserved in appearance, manner, and speech, especially in relation to sexual matters

MSN Encarta Dictionary

[On a side note, did you note the one definition "not overtly sexual"? I read a fascinating book entitled *Too Sexy Too Soon,* written by two secular authors, Dr. Levin and Dr. Kilbourne. I was shocked to read of parents dressing their girls like enticing movie stars and fashion models with hose, high heels and skimpy outfits! This book also gives examples of how the sexualization of our children has hit the mainstream. For example, little girls can now play with dolls that have hip-hugger undergarments and padded bras, and they can buy their own thong panties and padded bras that feature slang terms referring to sexual appearance and sex. Some adults just call it cute and harmless fun, but these authors and I call it dangerous.]

Webster's Old English dictionary from the 1800s used these words to describe modesty: "Not loosely or wantonly; decently, as to be modestly attired; to behave modestly." Notice that the meaning of the word *modest* has always been associated with dress *and* behavior.

We could give several more dictionary definitions, but the point that I want you to observe is that even the modern dictionaries have modesty associated with attitude, shyness and chastity. The Bible does this also. Modesty goes with purity and godliness quite well.

What Others Say About Modesty

I now want to introduce to my readers an excellent book entitled *What Is Modesty? Discovering the Truth* by

The Witness of Your Wardrobe

Michelle Brock. One of the things I like so much about this book is the emphasis placed on attitude and keeping a good balance in our view of modesty. I do not have the time to cover her book completely, but I would like to give you some quotes from a godly woman on this topic of modesty. (She accentuates each of these points with a flower, and they are beautiful to read!)

> Modesty is an attitude of humility that seeks to please God rather than man or self. It is characterized by restraint and self control and dignity in dress, speech and actions....Modesty is a product of pure thinking and is not determined by what you wear. You don't become modest simply by putting on a dress....Although it is not true that modesty equals clothing, it is true that what we wear and how we wear it can be modest or immodest.

Sometimes churches that take a biblical stand on modesty get a little pharisaical in their attitude if they are not careful. On the other hand, some pastors are so fearful of being pharisaical that they would rather tolerate immodesty than risk a bad attitude. Why should we have to choose? Listen to what Mrs. Brock says on this.

> A woman who dresses modestly because she fears God and delights to please Him wisely understands how much God hates prideful motives and pharisaical comparisons that exalt man rather than God. She doesn't abandon modest clothing to avoid being self-righteous. Rather, she abandons self-exalting motives and the critical spirit that is associated with pride and is so offensive to God....A humble woman may disagree with another's view of modesty, but she is careful how and when she communicates her opinion. And she understands that God works in different ways and times for each of us.

Does the world have any idea of what modesty is? I

went to the Physicians for Life web site (www.physicians-forlife.org) to read what they had to say about modesty. After viewing their site, I realized that it was mainly about stopping abortion and other serious consequences of immoral behavior. So why did they have an article on modesty? By the following quote, I think you will see how this web site tried to connect modesty and purity:

Women should dress in a way that veils the special mystery of [their] bodies that should be reserved for [their] spouse[s] alone. Modesty is closely related to the dignity of persons and [their] call to live out...chastity.

In his book *If You Really Loved Me,* Jason Evert also offers young women a view of modesty:

So what is modesty? It is not about looking as ugly as possible. It's about taking the natural beauty of womanhood and adorning it in a way that adequately reflects her true identity...her outfits, posture, and mannerisms don't distract from this. She's aware that her body is a priceless treasure.

This young man's quote is great, and I think that words like *chastity, identity* and *purity* sum up the thinking of these authors. Modesty in our dress and behavior is a reflection of a pure heart. Even though keeping high standards in the clothing you wear is often difficult in our fashion-frenzied world, it is possible and rewarding.

A young lady once told me about how liberated she felt when she determined to live a pure life of chastity. She had been struggling for years until she heard me teach on modesty and she made a decision to change her wardrobe. She said that after she made that change, she began attracting a different kind of friends and boys. Also, she was rejected by some of her past girlfriends, which was a blessing because they had been tempting her into intimate relationships with boys. Modest dress

The Witness of Your Wardrobe

changed her life and led to the right mate for her life. I rejoice!

I also discovered an article on modesty and its resurgence in the *USA TODAY* paper. Note how they described this new, modern modesty. Even the professor from liberal Wake Forest University seems to be on the right track.

Elizabeth Weise, *USA TODAY*

It's not out of the ordinary to see Muslim women in veils or chador, or Orthodox Jewish women wearing long skirts, long sleeves and wigs to cover their hair.

But it is unusual to see an American Christian woman covering her hair or adopting a distinctly modest style of dress that defines her as a person of faith in a secular society.

However, a small but seemingly growing number of women are adopting the garb of earlier times—form-concealing clothing...[Note the phrase "form-concealing," which I will refer to later.]

Modest dress is a much larger movement than hair covering within the Christian community, with shops and web sites devoted to long skirts, long-sleeved blouses, cover-up swimsuits and even bloomers for little girls. The desire is to find clothing that is traditionally feminine as well as modest.

Bill Leonard, dean of the Wake Forest University Divinity School, says, "It's possible that we could see a renewal of this distinctive dress in Christian families because it becomes its own kind of witness in a highly plural and increasingly secularized culture." [I think he is so right. This is a great time to be modest for Christ!]

18

3

SEPARATION AND SANCTIFICATION

What Are Separation and Sanctification?

It is important that we keep two Bible terms in mind with regard to topics that deal with standards or life-governing biblical principles: separation and sanctification. I will address the very word *standards* a little later. You may have had a bad experience in the past with some well-meaning zealot who beat you over the head with standards instead of touching your heart with them out of truth and love, but please don't let that term cause you to reject biblical principles outright. Sometimes Christians only think of the negative side of separation. Let's see how exciting these wonderful words really are in God's sight.

Please notice the Greek word for *separate* as found in II Corinthians 6:17:

> *"Wherefore come out from among them, and be ye separate, saith the Lord, and touch not the unclean thing; and I will receive you."*

God is commanding us to separate ourselves from that which defiles us, both worldly attitudes as well as actions. We know that because of what the Lord says right after this command. Often the Lord gives further explanation after giving a command. We do not have to have that; but just as a good parent often does, He wants to explain Himself. Second Corinthians 7:1 says,

> *"Having therefore these promises, dearly beloved, let us cleanse ourselves from all filthiness of the flesh and spirit, perfecting holiness in the fear of God."*

This verse makes it clear that God is not just talking about dressing right but having a right "spirit" that continues on to "holiness." God's goal is for us to be holy, godly and Christlike in our attitudes and actions!

Strong's Concordance defines the word "separate" as "to set off by boundary, i.e. (figuratively) limit, exclude, appoint, etc.: divide, separate, sever." It is a compound word made up of the Greek words that have the numbers 575 and 3724 in *Strong's Dictionary.* The numbers make it easier to look up the words without actually having to read the original languages.

Now I know that according to *Strong's Concordance* the Greek word for *Pharisee* means the "separated ones," but that word meaning "separated" isn't the same word God uses to tell us believers how to separate ourselves. We can be separated without being Pharisees when love is our motive.

Jesus clearly condemned the lifestyle of the Pharisees. He even condemned them for dressing in such a way that dishonestly tried to portray themselves as being spiritual when they were not. "They make broad their phylacteries, and enlarge the borders of their garments" [phylacteries: pieces of parchment containing sentences of the law] (Matthew 23:5). Clothing should be used as covering, but never a "cover-up."

Why do we want to separate from the "unclean" as II Corinthians 6:17 says? The simple answer is to please God—to please God so that we are separating ourselves *unto* God as well as *away* from the world!

Remember the second word I mentioned, *sanctification?* First Thessalonians 4:3 says:

> *"For this is the will of God, even your sanctification, that ye should abstain from fornication."*

This Greek word is also translated "holiness," and it describes the positive side of separation.

To be Christlike we must be separated as He was. Read how the Bible describes Him: "For such an high priest — became us, who is holy, harmless, undefiled, separate from sinners" (Hebrews 7:26). Notice it said, "separate from sinners," and yet we know He did not refrain from visiting them and eating with them on occasion. We know He did not become like them.

Oh, to have the balance of Christ to be loved by and respected of sinners without ever compromising God's precious Word! Somehow we must learn how to "fit in" in that Christlike way without being like them! This would include not dressing like them.

One thing I know for sure is that God wants his people to be holy and godly! Why do we fear that as if it were something that *repels* sinners? Being holy is nothing more than being Christlike. Never forget that Christ *attracted* sinners! Sinners flocked to Him. Only the hypocrites fled from Him! We do not need to be like the world to reach the world. We just need to be like Jesus! He came to save the lost, and He loves them so very, very much. He was compassionate yet didn't compromise with sin.

Two of my greatest fears in life are lack of compassion and compromise with sin! If I fail in either of these, then I will be unable to reach a lost and dying world. Lack of love and lack of purity will rob us of His precious power to reach the hurting. God save us from both of these frightful conditions!

The Witness of Your Wardrobe

Separation Is Pleasing to God

The rewards for practicing biblical separation are enormous! In fact, in the entire Bible I can find nothing else with greater promise of reward, except for being saved (Romans 10:9–13). How do we become more holy or separated? We become more holy in the same way that we get everything else from God—by faith!

> *"Wherefore come out from among them, and be ye separate, saith the Lord, and touch not the unclean thing; and I will receive you, And will be a Father unto you, and ye shall be my sons and daughters, saith the Lord Almighty."*—II Corinthians 6:17, 18.

When God says to the separated ones that He will "receive" us, He is saying that He can look on us with favor or be pleased with us. Oh, how I want to please Him!

Be careful as you read II Corinthians 6:18. It is not saying that we become His children through our separation but that He can fully reward us for our separation as a loving Father wants to do. I think we often miss the rewards of the family blessing by not being in the place of blessing.

What Past Christians Have Said About Separation

Please read the wonderful words of Charles Haddon Spurgeon, the great English preacher of the past, who wrote as a commentary on II Corinthians 6:18:

> Oh, that the Lord may make us, as a family, separated unto Himself. The great duty of believers in all ages is to maintain their character as a separate people, no more conformed to the world. May this family never fall into worldly fashions, amusements or pursuits, but be distinguished as following the Lord fully; so shall we be peculiarly dear to our Heavenly Father.

I don't think we can say it any better!

I would like to add one other verse for encouragement

toward holiness and separation from worldliness: "Abstain from all appearance of evil" (I Thessalonians 5:22). The word "appearance" is a good warning for us to be careful how we are seen by the world, whether it is clothes or even activities that are questionable. Read the old Albert Barnes commentary on this great verse and note he mentions dress also.

But there are also many things about which there may be some reasonable doubt. It is not quite easy to determine in the case what is right or wrong. The subject has not been fully examined, or the question of its morality may be so difficult to settle, that the mind may be nearly or quite balanced in regard to it.

There are many things which, in themselves, may not appear to us to be positively wrong but which are so considered by large and respectable portions of the community, and for us to do them would be regarded as inconsistent and improper. There are many things also in respect to which there is great variety of sentiment among mankind—where one portion would regard them as proper and another as improper. There are things also where, whatever may be our motive, we may be certain that our conduct will be regarded as improper. A great variety of subjects, such as those pertaining to dress, amusements, the opera, the ballroom, games of chance and hazard and various practices in the transaction of business, come under this general class, which, though on the supposition that they cannot be proved to be in themselves positively wrong or forbidden, have much the "appearance" of evil and will be so interpreted by others.

The safe and proper rule is to *lean always* to the side of virtue. In these instances, it may be certain that there will be no sin committed by abstaining; there may be by indulgence. No command of God or of propriety will be violated if we decline complying

23

with these customs; but, on the other hand, we may wound the cause of religion by yielding to what possibly is a mere temptation. No one ever does injury or wrong by abstaining from the pleasures of the ballroom, the theatre or a glass of wine; who can indulge in them without, in the view of large and respectable portions of the community, doing that which has the "appearance" at least "of evil"?

Why should we dilute what these great Bible teachers of old have said? Look at Spurgeon's comments on this verse also: "You cannot be too careful; if there be any manifestation of evil, however slight, shun it at once."

Separation in Ministry

Dr. Paul Chappell, a dear friend of mine, has written a great book on leadership, *Guided by Grace*. In that book he gives some of his guidelines for those who serve the Lord in a public role of leadership in his church. I remember hearing him share this a few years ago when I was at his Leadership Conference. He explained why he prefers to call his guidelines *leadership principles* instead of *standards*. His goal is not to compromise but to explain that with leadership come great privileges that make biblical separation worth it. When he got done teaching the class, I was looking for something else to give up for the Lord! I got excited! I encourage you to read the whole book, and especially chapters 18 and 19.

In defense of pastors teaching and insisting on some dress codes for those in leadership, let me make this observation from I Timothy 3:5:

"For if a man know not how to rule his own house, how shall he take care of the church of God?"

Note the phrase "take care of." The pastor is instructed to take care of the church of God. That instruction is never given to any other officer or leader in the church but the pastor. Thank God for those who help us in many tasks, but it is the job of the pastor to take care of the church of God, and it is obvious from other Scriptures that God isn't talking about the janitorial duties! A pastor should have liberty to lay down some rules for the house of God. I am not talking about being a dictator, but a leader. That is clearly his sphere of responsibility.

Men, your job is taking care of your house. Pastors can suggest and teach you about how to do this, but you make the decisions in your house (after consulting with your wife if you are a considerate husband). Are your house rules based on scriptural commands? Not all of them hopefully. Some will be based on scriptural *principles.* For instance, you decide what television programs to watch or even whether or not to have a television. The word television isn't even in the Bible, so there isn't a command, but you have a right to make rules about it.

Allow the pastor to have freedom to make rules based on the same concerns you have for your family: their safety and protection. Please recognize the similarities between your disagreeing with your pastor and your children's disagreeing with you! This is not easy, but please realize that pastors want the best for their family at God's house.

Pastors aren't the only ones to give us rules. In the Scriptures, the apostles also give us rules or commands that Jesus gave to them.

> *"Until the day in which he was taken up, after that he through the Holy Ghost had given commandments unto the apostles whom he had chosen."*—Acts 1:2.

The apostle Paul says, "If any man think himself to be a prophet, or spiritual, let him acknowledge that the things that I write unto you are the commandments of the Lord" (I Corinthians 14:37). We are not lawless, but these

The Witness of Your Wardrobe

laws lead us to holiness and Christlikeness. Jesus even said we could show our love by keeping His commandments (John 15:10).

4

THE RICHEST PASSAGE ON TRUE PURITY FOR CHRISTIAN WOMEN

"Likewise, ye wives, be in subjection to your own husbands; that, if any obey not the word, they also may without the word be won by the conversation of the wives; While they behold your chaste conversation coupled with fear. Whose adorning let it not be that outward adorning of plaiting the hair, and of wearing of gold, or of putting on of apparel; But let it be the hidden man of the heart, in that which is not corruptible, even the ornament of a meek and quiet spirit, which is in the sight of God of great price. For after this manner in the old time the holy women also, who trusted in God, adorned themselves, being in subjection unto their own husbands: Even as Sara obeyed Abraham, calling him lord: whose daughters ye are, as long as ye do well, and are not afraid with any amazement."—I Peter 3:1–6.

Now let's look at I Peter, chapter 3. Peter is writing to saved women who have unsaved husbands. I can't really imagine the pain of living with an unsaved spouse when you are saved and want desperately to serve and please God, but Peter gives these women some help. Does he tell them to leave that spouse in order to find their own happiness? No. Does he tell them to modernize their fashions to reach their full potential or become more like the world to reach their lost spouse? No. He tells them just the opposite. He calls on them to have a "chaste" life.

Look at *Strong's* definition of the word translated "chaste" and note that it is translated two other ways: "clear" and "pure" ["from the same as 40; properly, clean, i.e. (figuratively) innocent, modest, perfect:— chaste, clean, pure"]. The Greek root word for "chaste" is listed as number 40 in *Strong's*, which is the Greek word used most often in the KJB as "holy." Did you notice in the definition the word *modest?* We keep seeing it again and again.

The word "conversation" right beside "chaste" in verse 2 isn't just speaking about how we talk. That is generally how it is used today, but back in the 1600s, it meant your lifestyle or manner of living, and this included behavior.

It is absolutely amazing to me what Peter [God through His Word to Peter] does in this passage! He reaches all the way back nearly two thousand years in history to a woman who was the wife of the great patriarch Abraham and says that women are to emulate her (verses 4–6). That is old-fashioned! Peter even uses the phrase "in the old time." He says that women should seek to have the spirit or attitude of Sarah. She was a remarkable woman whose willingness to obey her husband led her to call him lord. In other words, her spirit of submission was greatly used of God.

> *"In like manner also, that women adorn themselves in modest apparel, with shamefacedness and sobriety; not with broided hair, or gold, or pearls, or costly array; But (which becometh women professing godliness) with good works."*—I Timothy 2:9, 10.

First Timothy 2:9 and 10 is another place in Scripture that refers to the Christian woman's dress and attitude. It is the only place this particular Greek word, *theosebeia*, is used for *godliness* in the whole New Testament. In all other places the Greek word *eusebeia* is used. *Theosebeia* is the strongest word for godliness that can be used, because the prefix is *theos,* which is the Greek word for God. (That is why we call the study of God "theology.") *Theosebeia* literally means "Godlikeness." Ladies, isn't it special that God wants you to show His likeness in a unique way? After considering verses 9 and 10, I think we can safely say that Christian ladies need to avoid looking flashy (too much make-up and/or jewelry) and acting fleshly (carnal or worldly).

Here is how a woman can literally show God's likeness in her life. First Timothy 2:9 and 10 stresses a woman's *attire* and her *attitude* but doesn't stop with those. Paul goes on to include her *actions,* "with good works," and reminds the woman she must also focus her *attention* on the home (Titus 2:5) and childbearing (I Timothy 2:15).

Look again at the beautiful language God uses in I Peter 3:1–5 to describe the truly feminine lady. She is not shabbily or sloppily adorned, but with modest clothing. Her ornaments are lasting and obvious because they stem from the heart, not from the latest fashions of the day. She has a "hidden" beauty that shows because she has the hidden Man (Christ) in her heart—Someone that the world of carnal feminism does not have.

Now some commentaries and some godly ladies think the "hidden man of the heart" is her husband. That will still fit in with the truly feminine lady because the modern feminists (I hate to use that word, but that is their label today) put themselves above their husbands and even their children. For the godly wife, Christ is the love of her heart, and her husband and children are the loves of her life.

The chaste lady described in this passage has something that God never uses to describe anybody else, something that is in God's sight "of great price"—a meek and quiet spirit! When you have something that is valuable in God's eyes, you have a special treasure! The God who uses gold to pave streets says that what this lady has is worth a "great price"! That is big!

In verse 6, godly ladies are called upon to follow the example of the godly Sarah who showed a high degree of submission to her husband. Peter reassures them to do this without being "afraid with any amazement."

What is amazement? When I looked this word up in my Bible dictionary, I found that the Greek word translated "amazement" is from a root word that is translated "terrify"—the idea of someone running away due to fear. Peter is saying to godly ladies that they shouldn't be afraid to have this kind of submissive spirit toward their husbands in particular and society in general.

Many Christian women are nervous or scared about dressing in such modest terms and are even offended at the thought of "obeying" their husbands. In fact, the phrase "to obey" is being deleted today from marriage vows by many modernized women. Christopher Reeve's wife, appearing on *Oprah*, was applauded loudly by the audience when she stated, "I refused to say the word 'obey' in our marriage vows." In today's world, it is popular to be unscriptural!

Now those reading this might think this male author is just a bigot, but let me ask you a question: Would you applaud children who said, "I refuse to say 'I will obey my parents'"? Of course not! Scripture says, "Children, obey your parents." But just like those children are rejecting Scripture, so are modern women rejecting Scripture. Read again of the example that God gives to wives today. "Even as Sara obeyed Abraham, calling him lord: whose daughters ye are, as long as ye do well, and are not afraid with any amazement" (I Peter 3:6). You can't be godly without a submissive spirit. This biblical principle is being rejected today.

Now does that mean that men have the right to abuse their wives and make their lives miserable? No! Men don't have that right any more than parents have the right to abuse and mistreat their children. Abuse of power and mistreatment of others have always been problems, but they don't negate God's principles of leadership and submission.

Looking at verse 6, you may wonder, "How would Sarah have dressed? How have ladies dressed in general over the ages?" I think that Peter's reference to the "old time" would give us the liberty and even encouragement to look back at the history of women's dress. We will have to start with biblical times, since that is where Peter's frame of reference began. Both the Bible and history teach us that women in Bible times wore robes or robe-like garments. How did our clothing change from Bible times to now? Over the next few chapters, we will be looking at how and why dress has changed and whether or not these changes are scriptural.

I know a person can take the exact same historical facts that another person reads and make them say something completely different. I will admit that I do have a bias because I am a preacher who has taken a definite position on dress in my ministry over many years. I promise you that I will be as careful as I can with the facts.

5

I AM NOT CONVICTED!

Have you noticed the last few years how easily people are "convicted" of using tobacco? Until the last few years they smoked, but then their children started pleading with them to quit; and doctors who used to smoke themselves quit and told their patients they had better quit also. The states then started making people stop smoking on the airplanes and subways, in the restaurants, etc., and this all led people to conviction, even if not exactly the same kind we preachers would have preferred. Still we are thankful that God's people are taking better care of God's body!

One the most common excuses for immodest dress that some Christians and others use is this: "I am not convicted about the way I dress!" I have actually had a teen say that to me while wearing tight-fitting jeans and a top that was so short that her navel was showing. And I believe that she was being truthful! I don't think she was convicted about what she was wearing. Here is the story:

One Sunday evening, she and her whole family happened to visit our church during one of my two messages a year on the subject of dress. They were offended—or angered might be the better word—even though I always try to be kind and understanding in those messages. They expressed their feelings to another family who shared them with me.

I went by their house a few days later to see how they were doing. I had not chosen the message for them. It had been planned long in advance and even announced two weeks before. They brought up the topic by saying that they thought God looked on the heart, not on the outside. I replied that God does say some things about our outward dress in the Bible, some of which I had brought up in the message. The teen girl dressed so immodestly then made the statement that I quoted in the first paragraph: "I'm not convicted!"

Why wasn't she convicted? She wasn't convicted for the same reason that many other ladies and girls are not convicted, even though they wear some of the most blatantly immodest clothing ever known in our world's history. They have been CONDITIONED!

In this matter of modesty, we had society on our side at one time, but not anymore. At one time there were people in our society who had the influence of grandmothers who agreed with what the preacher said about modesty, but not anymore. Grandmothers today are often dressed as immodestly as the granddaughters! (This is when I can be thankful for being blind so I don't have to look at some of those sights!) However, God's people must not follow society's ideas when they dress their bodies—which we all know are *His* temple! As you read this book, please don't cast off everything simply because you are not convicted. You may just be conditioned!

In fact, we all need to be careful lest we allow the secular media world of movies, television and magazines to condition or accustom us to seeing immodesty. I think most Christians underestimate how much we have all been influenced by our society.

I Am Not Convicted!

When Christian speaker Nancy Leigh DeMoss* addressed a group of ladies on the topics of dress and modesty, she noted that many of them had come to think their dress was modest when they compared their clothing to the latest fashions pictured in the newest fashion magazines. Compared to the women in the magazines, almost all the women in her audience felt they were modest. Later in the seminar, the ladies realized they had become so accustomed to seeing immodest dress that they had adapted to that style.

That is an example of society's conditioning us, and Satan uses that technique in many areas of our lives. We watch television shows with more and more violence and sexual innuendos simply because we have become accustomed to them, and we listen to music that is increasingly worldly as we grow accustomed to questionable lyrics.

Let us beware of one of Satan's most effective weapons today: relativism. Relativism is "a theory, especially in ethics or aesthetics, that conceptions of truth and moral values are not absolute but are *relative* to the persons or groups holding them."

Philosophy

Another definition that I found is "the doctrine that no ideas or beliefs are universally true but that all are, instead, 'relative'—that is, their validity depends on the circumstances in which they are applied."

American Heritage New Dictionary of Cultural Literacy, Third Edition

Notice the phrase "no ideas or beliefs are universally true." These words eliminate one of the most strongly held beliefs in historic Christianity: there is one absolute Truth that is to be universally held and accepted—the Word of God. It is absolute truth for all mankind in any culture and under any circumstance. To think "what's true for you may not be true for me" must not become the new standard for our dress or actions! May we be able to state the same thing the Psalmist stated in Psalm 119:128: "Therefore I esteem all thy precepts concerning all things to be right; and I hate every false way."

I think some ladies accidentally dress unscripturally because they are just not careful. Carefulness is commanded to all believers, although the word most often used for carefulness is translated "sober" or "vigilant" in our King James Bibles. One of the times the English word *careful* is used in the KJB in a positive sense is in Titus 3:8:

> *"These things I will that thou affirm constantly, that they which have believed in God might be careful to maintain good works."*

We need to be careful not only to avoid that which is wrong about our dress choices but also to do what is right! Carefulness or soberness is very important in the last days before the Lord comes. First Peter 4:7 says:

> *"But the end of all things is at hand: be ye therefore sober, and watch unto prayer."*

Let us never forget that Satan is after us. We must be careful lest we fall! Remember I Peter 5:8:

> *"Be sober, be vigilant; because your adversary the devil, as a roaring lion, walketh about, seeking whom he may devour."*

Don't think he won't use dress associations and attractions!

*From everything I have read by and about Sister DeMoss as well as from the personal testimony of those who know her, I think she is a very godly lady. In fact, I ordered the CDs on dress and modesty that she produced from her broadcasts, and I like her "Style Quiz" on her web site, *Revive Our Hearts,* where she gives good principles for dress. She is not considered a fundamentalist in the same sense of the word that some of us would define the term. I say "us" because I consider myself to be a Christian who sincerely and unashamedly believes in the fundamentals of the Christian faith. I like to say I am "positively fundamental." I think Sister DeMoss's core beliefs would be very similar to ours with some differences that are minor compared to those who define themselves as liberals in the Christian world.

For instance, those fundamentalists with whom I am familiar use the Old King James Bible as opposed to other translations. We believe very wise, intelligent and diligent men, such as the late Dr. Henry Morris, showed us the differences in the translations are real. Our fundamentalist colleges and Bible institutes are known, for the most part, for having conservative views on such issues as dress, dating and other social issues. I am so thankful that in these days some evangelicals such as Miss DeMoss—I think that is the term she would prefer—and a few others are speaking out so boldly on the issue of modesty!

6
A MATTER OF THE HEART

In the Home

Nancy DeMoss has written what I consider to be one of the most discerning booklets on dress. It is entitled *Cultivating a Pure Heart: Becoming a Woman of Discretion in a Sensual World*. One of the things that I appreciate about this booklet is the biblical and unique way that Sister DeMoss shows that the heart of a wife belongs in the home and what an impact godly wives have had on our whole society and culture. On page 18 she says, "The greatest spiritual, moral and emotional protection a woman will ever experience is found when she is content to stay within her God-appointed sphere. This does not mean that she never leaves her house, but rather that her heart is rooted in her home and she puts her family's needs above all other interests and pursuits." Now, only a lady can say that with authority—and then only a godly lady who is using Scripture to support her position! If I or any other man said that, we would be crucified.

In Our Country

Sister DeMoss also quotes John Adams, the second president of the United States, who recognized the incredible influence of women, not only on their own homes, but on the entire character of a nation. He said, "From all that I have read of history and government and human life and manners, I have drawn this conclusion: that the manners of women were the most infallible barometer to ascertain the degree of morality and virtue of a nation. The Jews, the Greeks, the Romans, the Swiss, the Dutch, all lost their public spirit and their republican forms of government when they lost the modesty and domestic virtues of their women."

Yet another quote from her booklet says, "In recent years we have seen the power of foolish women to tear down and destroy the moral sensitivities and fiber of an entire nation. We can all think of high-profile women—entertainers, politicians, wives of public figures—whose philosophies and lifestyles have wielded an enormous, negative influence on our entire culture. [I agree wholeheartedly!] We have little comprehension of the meaning or importance of such old-fashioned words as **wholesome, modest, discreet** and **chaste.** [emphasis hers]"

Our country experienced a philosophical and psychological shift years ago. The liberal organization called NOW (National Organization for Women), which opposes all biblical role models for both men and women and is revered by today's feminists, came into being around that time and published the infamous book *The Feminine Mystique* by Betty Friedan. It was a bestseller.

Read this assessment of that book that I found in *Wikipedia*. "According to *The New York Times* obituary of Friedan in 2006, it *[The Feminine Mystique]* 'ignited the contemporary women's movement in 1963 and, as a result, permanently transformed the social fabric of the United States and countries around the world' and 'is widely regarded as one of the most influential nonfiction books of the twentieth century.'"

According to Betty Friedan's book, a woman's dressing

40

as she pleases and aborting her babies were a part of her "universal human right." In chapter 12, entitled "Progressive Dehumanization: The Comfortable Concentration Camp," Friedan compared being tied to a home and having to put the word *housewife* on an application to the conditions of being a prisoner in a concentration camp. She used faulty data, such as pieces of Freudian thinking and the thinking of other so-called experts of her day, to make women feel they were truly unhappy with the role of womanhood as presented in the Bible. She believed that the voice women should listen to was the voice from within, not the Word of God. She says, "Even the best psychoanalyst can only give her the courage to listen to her own voice....Every woman has to listen to her own inner voice to find her identity."

At the time I am writing this (September 16, 2008), I am looking at a copy of the *USA TODAY* newspaper. America is just a few weeks away from the general presidential election, and the feminist movement is very much in the forefront of this election because one of the former candidates, Hillary Rodham Clinton, is a very strong liberal feminist. In fact, Mrs. Clinton refused to change her last name after her marriage to Bill Clinton until their political aspirations simply demanded it of her and her husband several years ago. She associates openly with NOW and is very vocal about being pro-abortion. Republican nominee for president, John S. McCain, has chosen a woman named Sarah Palin as his choice for vice president. There is a stark contrast between these two women.

Sarah Palin belongs to a pro-life organization called Feminists for Life. Regardless of whether or not you feel she should be a political mom or even be placed in the office of the vice presidency, I admire her for being feminine in dress and demeanor and being willing to stand against abortion unashamedly. Liberals believe in

The Witness of Your Wardrobe

abortion on demand at any stage, yet Mrs. Palin expressed disapproval some years ago for her own husband's support of partial-birth abortion. (That type of abortion is the most reprehensible and inhuman type known to man. It basically allows the doctor to pull the unborn child—remember that *child* is the term God uses in His Word to describe pregnancy—partially out of the womb so that the doctor can use an instrument to make a hole in the head and suction out the brains, causing death.) A truly godly woman would *never* support the killing of unborn children!

Here is a portion of one of the two letters to the editor on this day:

> What perfect timing—we just celebrated the eighty-eighth anniversary of women winning the right to vote, and along comes Sarah Palin, cutting right through forty years of feminist orthodoxy in two weeks. No wonder some feminists hate her....Palin recaptures the historic position and collective sentiment of early women's rights campaigners such as Susan B. Anthony, Elizabeth Cady Stanton and the very first woman presidential candidate, Victoria Woodhull, who uniformly opposed abortion. Alice Paul, author of the original 1923 Equal Rights Amendment, denounced the abortion-rights position of later ERA advocates, calling abortion "the ultimate exploitation of women." One thing is clear in this election cycle: American women are most definitely not an unthinking, monolithic "her" that can be manipulated by the likes of NARAL Pro-Choice America and the National Organization for Women....The historical record is clear: classic feminism is pro-woman and pro-life."

The second letter, which is decidedly against Mrs. Palin, is entitled "VP Pick Halts Progress."

Years ago, people in marketing realized women's strength in numbers and targeted them in advertising campaigns. Now, with the future of our country at stake and with the success of Hillary Clinton's candidacy, Republicans see the power of women to win this election. So they chose a 'skirt' for their nominee for vice president. [Quotation marks are hers, not mine.] With the choice of Palin, the Republicans have insulted women and have set back feminism. Palin is a virtual poster girl whose appeal, ironically, is to men....This is not the woman for whom feminists have waited....The most frightening part is that Palin's beliefs are the antithesis of what feminists have fought for. Most important on that list is her stance on *Roe v. Wade* and the right to choose....This woman would set feminism back half a century.

Liberals are determined to make homemakers feel as if they are missing out on something. Betty Friedan, the author that I referred to earlier whose liberal views really led women farther to the left, makes it clear that even Martha Stewart is detrimental to her cause simply for making it appear as though women can truly find happiness and fulfillment by being what the Bible calls "keepers at home" (Titus 2:5).

Also, concerning the effects of the liberal feminist movement, Nancy DeMoss shares this insight from her mother: "She didn't know she was supposed to be unhappy until people told her she shouldn't have to deal with all the demands of her busy household." So Martha Stewart's teaching of ladies how to decorate, cook, etc., in the home is too much a part of the ideal of the pre-NOW era. I think it is a lie of Satan to cast aside the biblical role model which includes modesty in dress and demeanor also.

In Our Churches

Because of the psychological shift we've seen in our

country, we as Christians excuse, tolerate and justify behavior that would have been unthinkable a generation ago. I think this is true especially in the area of dress, and this isn't just a problem that occurs outside of fundamentalist circles. I must admit that it is happening in our fundamentalist churches and schools. During the years that I traveled before my blindness, I was shocked by the dress and behavior in some of our churches. In fact, one blessing of being blind is that when I travel, I do not have to observe some of the blatant immodesty in public places.

Commenting on the attire and the heart of the foolish woman in Proverbs 7:10, Sister DeMoss says, "The attire...[is] (the outward manifestation) and 'having a crafty heart' [is] (the inward heart that produces the outward manifestation)....Though this woman is not a harlot, she is dressed like one. Suggestive, seductive clothing is one of the traps she uses to lure the young man. Immodest clothing is a mark of the foolish woman; modest dress is a mark of a wise, godly woman. **Few women today, even in our churches, seem to understand the meaning or importance of modesty. [emphasis mine]**"

Let me hasten to say that I expect lost women to be unaware of some of the issues of modesty, especially biblical modesty. However, I do not think it wise for churches to advertise, "Dress as you please." The house of worship should still be looked at with respect, but we must allow women who have grown up in such an immoral society to learn what is right. I have told some of our fundamentalist brethren that if they do not have some immodestly dressed ladies in their services, they are probably not reaching out to the hurting people in their community as actively as they should. We must love hurting people no matter how they are dressed, but love them enough to teach them patiently what God says after they come to know the Lord.

7
THE LANGUAGE OF CLOTHING!

Clothes have a language all their own. Historians, psychologists and a host of people from all the sciences of life have looked at this subject and have given us some very clear and concise principles and viewpoints. The very title of one secular book that my wife had to "clean up" for me speaks volumes: *What You Wear Can Change Your Life.* You had better believe that too! The world truly believes you can change your life by changing your wardrobe, but many Christians and even Christian leaders say otherwise. Many authors and researchers clearly believe that people both send and receive messages through their dress. Some of the messages are intentional and some are unintentional, but those messages are still being sent!

Remember the letters to the editor from the *USA TODAY?* Did you catch the reference to her "skirt" in the letter criticizing Sarah Palin? Hillary's campaign was known as the "pant suit brigade," yet Mrs. Palin has appeared on stage at this point almost entirely in dresses or skirts. Clothes really are a part of the package to feminists, and they want it to be known that they will dress like men because they desire to do so. (Please understand this: I do not think that every woman who ever wears pants or pant suits is showing her agreement with liberal

The Witness of Your Wardrobe

feminists. Remember that one point I am trying to make in this section of the book is that many Christians are unknowingly going along with a movement they really don't agree with. Many are godly women that are unaware of scriptural teaching, the goals of liberal feminists or both. PLEASE DON'T TAKE WHAT I AM SAYING AS AN ACCUSATION! I WANT US TO LEARN AND GROW!)

The Unisex Movement

This movement of women wanting to become more like men was also known as the "unisex" movement. Cross-dressing was a part of that whole movement. Although the beginning of the radical change started with women dressing more and more like men, it is now making inroads into males dressing more feminine. Most Christian women would never want to contribute to the homosexual movement, but dressing carelessly and following the crowd can certainly contribute to this unscriptural cause. Remember that your clothing sends messages to others.

The world has coined the term "unisex," not pastors. This term was used by the feminists on purpose. A more modern term for unisex dressing is androgynous. Androgynous is defined as:

1. having the characteristics or nature of both male and female

2. neither specifically feminine nor masculine < the *androgynous* pronoun *them* >, suitable to or for either sex < *androgynous* clothing >

3. having traditional male and female roles obscured or reversed

Merriam-Webster OnLine Dictionary.

Read the following quote that I found at a web site called "Sixties Central":

Unisex clothing was a natural progression from changes in both women's and men's roles in society. When looking ahead, many fashion designers predicted that people would wear unisex clothing in the future, and ever since the 1960s it has been a valid look for both men and women.

Some women began to wear men's jeans and T-shirts in the late 1950s. In the 1960s jeans became a growing cult, and by the end of the decade this look was widespread. With men growing their hair long and with females having boyish figures, it became difficult to distinguish a boy from a girl in the '60s. Mass manufacturing of clothing meant it was possible for couples to walk around in exactly the same outfits. Both boys and girls wore long hair, headbands, worn-out jeans and sloppy casual outfits.

This statement, as well as many other historical references, clearly demonstrates that the unisex (androgynous) thinking came from an unscriptural philosophy that has permeated our society and our churches to such an extent that we must now remind ourselves why we do or don't do certain things. We *do not* want to dress in certain ways because dressing that way would give our approval to the thinking behind this unscriptural movement. On the other hand, we *do* want to dress in certain ways because dressing in those ways would show our support of biblical principles.

Hollywood's Contribution

The first real and open use of such clothing in America's public eye was done by an actress named Marlene Dietrich under the guidance of Hollywood director Josef von Sternberg in the 1930s. (Some other countries experimented with cross-dressing on the stage, particularly Nazi Germany.) This Hollywood team made a bold move in 1935 in a film called *The Devil Is a Woman.*

The Witness of Your Wardrobe

This film was advertised with a picture of Dietrich in male clothing with cigarette smoke rising toward her face.

The following are some excerpts from the book *Dressing the Part,* which describes in detail the role Miss Dietrich played in influencing society to dress in a different style than it ever had before.

> Adolph Zukor, Paramount's studio chief, spoke of how the trend had begun. "Marlene's indifference to publicity was a major reason why millions of Americans today wear slacks. At one point our publicity department decided that new press photographs of Dietrich were needed. 'I'm loafing around in slacks,' she told Blake McVeigh, the publicity man assigned to get the pictures. 'If you want to shoot me this way, all right'....She posed in her trousers and...the photographs were in great demand by the press. All over the country the stores were raided for their small supplies of women's slacks. The rage was on.

Margaret Bailey sees the acceptance of slacks into public life as one of the major innovative fashion occurrences of the thirties..."She [Marlene Dietrich] was the first to wear slacks in public in 1931 in Hollywood, although everyone wore them on the studio lot. It is ironic that a woman renowned for her femininity would launch a new vogue of fashionable masculinity."

Since we were discussing dress and the feminist movement earlier, I also want to mention that *Dressing the Part* makes this statement: "Cross-dressing can also be viewed as a political statement that utilizes costume to redefine the female self." A phrase often used in this book in describing the motives behind the cross-dressing is "sexual ambiguity." Keep in mind that these are not preachers but the producers and profiteers of a new fashion that describe the slacks as male attire and cross-dressing. I and other pastors have been accused of making up these terms to fit our views, but, in actuality, this was the world's view at one time. Christians have just forgotten it, and we need to be reminded of these matters.

8

THE UNISEX MOVEMENT
AND THE BIBLE

*"The woman shall not wear that which pertaineth unto
a man, neither shall a man put on a woman's garment: for
all that do so are abomination unto the LORD thy God."*—
Deuteronomy 22:5.

Please set aside all the arguments against using a principle found in an Old Testament passage to guide us today. We all know we can set out to make the Scriptures teach something they do not teach, but that is not what I am trying to do. If you are reading this verse for the first time, what does it make you think right now—right now before you hear or read anything else about it? What visual determination are you making to try to picture its meaning?

I experimented with some teens and adults who had admitted to me they had never heard or read this verse in their lives. After reading it, what response did they give me? Here are some samples:

"It means men and women are not supposed to dress alike, I think."

"It must have something to do with homosexuality, stuff like cross-dressing."

The Witness of Your Wardrobe

"God doesn't want us to try to look like another sex, but I don't know what that means exactly. Like, who says what is a woman's or man's garment? Do you know?"

"It must mean that in the Old Testament God didn't want men and women dressing alike, but I am glad we are living in the New Testament!"

Did you get any connection or theme running through those answers? I did. God, at some point or time, did not let women and men dress alike. Why do we try to twist and contort this verse or just forget about it since it is in the Old Testament? The answer, I think (and I am sure some of you will disagree), is that this verse is controversial and could possibly indict too many people who have knowingly or accidently crossed a line somewhere in the area of dress. I cannot tell you and will not claim to know every article of clothing, then or now, that God had in mind. None of us know. I do know that God cares about our dressing to please Him rather than to disappoint Him.

Three Kinds of Clothing

Most pastors, Bible teachers and Christians think that there are only two styles of dress found in the Bible: male and female. This is a mistaken viewpoint. You see, when the controversial Deuteronomy 22:5 was written, both men and women wore robes. That means that there are three types of clothing: male, female and neutral. However, those neutral pieces of clothing are decorated to make them either male or female.

Robes happen to be one of those neutral articles of clothing that are still used today. In fact, I have a robe-like garment called an overcoat, and so does my wife, but mine isn't pink and doesn't have fluff around the collar. A robe can be made to look feminine or masculine.

Shoes are neutral. Both sexes wear them, and yet there

are some shoes that I wouldn't be caught dead in! Do you see what I am saying?

People who oppose clothing guidelines say that some clothes are okay for both genders to wear because they are neutral. However, they are not taking into account the fact that these clothes are made to look either masculine or feminine.

Many people say sincerely, although I think mistakenly, "If men and women both wore robes in Bible days, why can't we all wear pants?" To me that is like saying, "They all wore shoes in Bible days, so we can all wear hats!" They have nothing to do with each other. We have much historical evidence from secular society as well as Christian history to prove that pants were a specifically male garment adopted by females. The very fact that they were designed with a zipper shows that they were made with men in mind.

Some excuse this verse by saying the word for "man" is *geber* instead of *adam*. *Geber* is sometimes translated "mighty," and *Strong's Concordance* says that it speaks of a soldier or warrior. Thus, some say that this verse was just forbidding women from dressing up as soldiers. Now I admit that I approach this verse with a bias, but I think that argument is ridiculous! If you look up the meaning of the word *adam*, you find it is a much more general word for human beings. So instead of using *adam*, God used a word that would be easier for the reader to identify, one that refers specifically to a man.

Several of the Hebrew words in this verse can have different meanings, but the translators felt the context was clear, and so do I. Let us not start changing Scriptures and contorting texts to make them say something just to agree with our views. Remember, I am not dogmatically saying all women's slacks are specifically included in this verse, but I do believe that many are and that the New

Testament principles of dress would make the rest of them suspect, to say the least.

Does Deuteronomy 22:5 Still Apply to Christians Today?

I want to answer some arguments that many well-meaning and sincere Christians use to say that this verse doesn't apply to us today and, at the same time, tell why I believe the *principle* behind this verse still applies. I believe the principle still stands for the following reason: several immoral or sinful actions are condemned in the Old Testament, and we still consider them to be wrong even though they are never mentioned by Christ or any other New Testament writer, or perhaps they are less clearly mentioned or described with different terminology in the New Testament.

I do want you to know this: I believe that God has done away with some commands and warnings in the Old Testament since the death, burial and resurrection of Jesus Christ and the writings of the New Testament, but I still believe there are many moral teachings God meant for all mankind for all time! I think we all still condemn these Old Testament things that I now list in that category.

> "When thou art come into the land which the LORD thy God giveth thee, thou shalt not learn to do after the abominations of those nations. There shall not be found among you any one that maketh his son or his daughter to pass through the fire, or that useth divination, or an observer of times, or an enchanter, or a witch, Or a charmer, or a consulter with familiar spirits, or a wizard, or a necromancer. For all that do these things are an abomination unto the LORD: and because of these abominations the LORD thy God doth drive them out from before thee."— Deuteronomy 18:9–12.

We are not as familiar with all of these words as people were in earlier times, so let me explain some of them. They all have to do with practices that have resurfaced today. For instance, making a child pass through the fire is still in practice by heathen nations who kill innocent children for a false god's pleasure. Can that ever be right in any generation? No, yet God did not repeat this command directly or even indirectly in the New Testament.

I have a biblical right to associate false gods with making children pass through a fire because several Old Testament passages connect the two together. In Leviticus 18:21, the Israelites were warned not to pass a child through the fire: "And thou shalt not let any of thy seed pass through the fire to Molech."

What amazed me was how often the other sins listed in Deuteronomy, chapter 18, occurred when a future king practiced child sacrifice. Note just a couple of incidents. In II Kings, chapter 16, a young king named Ahaz started practicing child sacrifice and "made his son to pass through the fire" as told in verse 3. It was not long before the people followed this practice—a reason why we need godly rulers. In chapter 17, the people were no longer just committing child sacrifice. Look at the list of sins and see if they do not sound familiar.

> *"And they left all the commandments of the LORD their God, and made them molten images, even two calves, and made a grove, and worshipped all the host of heaven, and served Baal. And they caused their sons and their daughters to pass through the fire, and used divination and enchantments, and sold themselves to do evil in the sight of the LORD, to provoke him to anger"*—II Kings 17:16, 17.

God had warned them in verse 13 to turn from these practices and then judged them greatly. You would think that Israel would have never allowed that again, but later came Manasseh who did the same thing with the same dire consequences (21:1–6).

The Witness of Your Wardrobe

I wish the world could understand the reason why most Christians could never vote for a "pro-choice" candidate who accepts the practice—yea, the slaughter—of sacrificing unborn children to the false gods of pleasure and money. Any nation that mistreats the innocent among them will most surely suffer God's judgment. Gary Schwer, a pastor friend of mine, sent me an advertisement for an Arizona abortion clinic that says, "No Fetus Can Beat Us!" How low can we sink? Read how Manasseh caused his people to practice the sacrifice of children and worse:

> "And he caused his children to pass through the fire in the valley of the son of Hinnom: also he observed times, and used enchantments, and used witchcraft, and dealt with a familiar spirit, and with wizards: he wrought much evil in the sight of the LORD, to provoke him to anger"—II Chronicles 33:6.

Do you see how one practice leads to others? Child sacrifice, witchcraft, familiar spirits and observers of times are all mentioned in these passages. We have in America those who have televised their own contacts with dead relatives (consulting with familiar spirits).

Referring to the Deuteronomy 18 passage, necromancers are not just consulters with the dead, but are those who practice perverted acts with dead bodies. Here is how up-to-date this is. Recently, an employee of a funeral home was arrested when relatives discovered some of the perverted ways their loved ones' bodies were being treated.

The astrologers of our day (observers of times) have people conducting their whole lives around some sign in the sky instead of reading the Bible, praying and seeking godly counsel. Since Jesus and Paul didn't mention these acts, are they all right now? I hope you are helping your people see these dangers even though they are not clearly condemned in the New Testament.

Another clear teaching from the Old Testament that is not mentioned in the New Testament is the sin of bestiality.

"Neither shalt thou lie with any beast to defile thyself therewith: neither shall any woman stand before a beast to lie down thereto: it is confusion"—Leviticus 18:23.

This is so abhorrent to me that I only mention it because God does so in His Word. Bestiality is a growing trend, so I am told, in pornography. I recently saw on the news (with the aid of my goggles) that a young man was arrested after some young people saw him committing lewd acts with two animals. God have mercy! Now do you see why I think it is not possible to throw out all Old Testament passages simply because we live in the New Testament age?

Pornography in general is another thing that is mentioned more clearly in the Old Testament than in the New Testament. In my thinking, pornography degrades women and all of society, and the Old Testament certainly spells out what it is and why it is wrong. In the New Testament, Jesus expands the thought by saying that intentional lustful thoughts are considered to be adultery (Matthew 5:28).

Let me give you one more major sin mentioned by Moses but not called by the same name in the New Testament. That is the sin of sodomy. While this word is not in the New Testament, I think it is part of what is meant in phrases like "vile affections," "lust of uncleanness" and sometimes "fornication." Then there is God's clear condemnation of homosexual practices, using other terms, in Romans 1:26 and 27.

"For this cause God gave them up unto vile affections: for even their women did change the natural use into

that which is against nature: And likewise also the men, leaving the natural use of the woman, burned in their lust one toward another; men with men working that which is unseemly, and receiving in themselves that recompence of their error which was meet."

The failure to use the same terms in the New Testament in describing something condemned in the Old Testament does not mean that we can ignore what Moses said because we are living under the New Testament.

Most preachers do not honestly believe in throwing out Deuteronomy 22:5 completely anyway. For instance, most preachers would object to the wearing of flowery dresses by men. We all believe *something* about that verse; we just may not believe the same things. Let us both be more loving with what we say about the other side!

9

PAST PREACHERS ON CROSS-DRESSING

When people today think of Deuteronomy 22:5, one of their first thoughts is cross-dressing. It may interest you to know that this is what early preachers believed this verse was talking about, long before the issue became widespread and controversial. Read some of these observations from many years ago.

The Jamieson-Fausset-Brown Commentary that was written in the 1870s says this:

Deuteronomy 22:5–12. THE SEX TO BE DISTINGUISHED BY APPAREL. "The woman shall not wear that which pertaineth unto a man, neither shall a man put on a woman's garment"—Though disguises were assumed at certain times in heathen temples, it is probable that a reference was made to unbecoming levities practised in common life. They were properly forbidden; for the adoption of the habiliments of the one sex by the other is an outrage on decency, obliterates the distinctions of nature by fostering softness and effeminacy in the man, impudence and boldness in the woman as well as levity and hypocrisy in both; and, in short, it opens the door to an influx of so many evils that all who wear the dress of another sex are pronounced an "abomination unto the LORD."

The Witness of Your Wardrobe

C. H. Spurgeon, a great Baptist preacher of the late 1800s, also connected this verse to cross-dressing and applied it to his age directly. He said, "All indelicacy is to be shunned. No idea of merriment can excuse that which has a lewd appearance." After researching what he could have meant by "no idea of merriment can excuse," I am convinced that he was denouncing the Shakespearean plays popular in his day where men dressed as women on the stage because of the culture's condemnation of women's being involved in theatrical settings. He was saying there is no excuse for dressing like the opposite sex even for fun in a performance. Pretty strong, isn't it?

A note concerning this verse in the Geneva Bible of 1599 says, "For that [cross-dressing] alters the order of nature and shows that you despise God." Cross-dressing goes against nature, which is precisely what I (along with many others) am saying.

Adam Clark's Commentary, which also dates back one hundred years or more, believes this verse probably has a two-fold idea: one of an idolatrous practice in the Old Testament days and the obvious one we have all stated. He says,

> The close-shaved gentleman may at anytime appear like a woman in the female dress, and the woman appear as a man in the male's attire. Were this to be tolerated in society, it would produce the greatest confusion. Clodius, who dressed himself like a woman that he might mingle with the Roman ladies in the feast of the Bona Dea, was universally execrated.

He even gave an example from his day of a man with perverted desires and his universal condemnation.

John Wesley, the Methodist founder, made it clear how strongly he felt about this verse. He writes,

V. 5. Shall not wear—Namely, ordinarily or unnec-
essarily, for in some cases this may be lawful, as to
make an escape for one's life. Now this is forbidden,
both for decency's sake, that men might not con-
found those sexes which God hath distinguished, that
all appearance of evil might be avoided, such change
of garments carrying a manifest sign of effeminacy in
the man, of arrogance in the woman, of lightness and
petulancy in both; and also to cut off all suspicions
and occasions of evil, which this practice opens a
wide door to.

Matthew Henry's Commentary, one of the greatest and
most revered commentaries of all time, says essentially
the same:

[The distinction of sexes by the] apparel is to be
kept up for the preservation of our own and our
neighbour's chastity (Deuteronomy 22:5). Nature
itself teaches that a difference be made between
them in their hair (I Corinthians 11:14), and by the
same rule in their clothes, which therefore ought not
to be confounded, either in ordinary wear or occa-
sionally. To befriend a lawful escape or concealment
it may be done, but whether for sport or in the acting
of plays is justly questionable. Some think it [this
verse] refers to the idolatrous custom of the Gentiles:
in the worship of Venus, women appeared in armour
and men in women's clothes; this, as other such
superstitious usages, is here said to be an abomination to the Lord. It forbids the confounding of the dis-
positions and affairs of the sexes: men must not be
effeminate nor do the women's work in the house;
nor must women be viragoes, pretend to teach or
usurp authority (I Timothy 2:11,12). Probably this
confounding of garments had been used to gain
opportunity of committing uncleanness and is therefore forbidden, for those that would be kept from sin

must keep themselves from all occasions of it and approaches to it.

You may have noticed that while some of these commentators mentioned cross-dressing in reference to pagan practices, none of them mentioned *only* the pagan practices. Yet, some modern-day teachers have taken hold of this idolatrous aspect to the exclusion of the clearer meaning altogether.

A somewhat prolific evangelist from California named Ralph Woodrow who holds preachers like me in disdain says this verse is referring to "cultic transvestism" where the participants dressed as the opposite sex in idolatrous rites. So he does away with any contextual meaning for our day unless you are idolatrous or a woman soldier.

By the way, in his booklet *Women's Adornment—What Does the Bible Really Say?* he says that in I Corinthians 11:1–16, Paul is not dealing with long hair on men and short hair on women. He takes the liberty to change the whole meaning by drastically changing the King James translation to fit his interpretation.

"Next, Paul appeals to an argument from nature. What the KJV translators give as a question—'Doth not even nature itself teach you, that, if a man have long hair, it is a shame unto him?'—could just as correctly be translated: 'Even nature does not teach you, that, if a man have long hair, it is a shame unto him.'"

I have a problem with his changing the translation in general, but also specifically here, because the whole context is contrasting the difference in hair length between the two sexes. Sometimes liberals like this man say we twist Scripture to make our points. I know all of us are in danger of reading more into a text than we should to prove our points, but this is ridiculous!

He even calls the warnings of both Paul and Peter about

excessive jewelry a "Hebrew idiom" that takes out the natural meaning. He goes contrary to all the commentaries I read, with the exception of one, and certainly against every fundamentalist I have ever read.

I believe he also showed some ignorance when he made a sweeping statement concerning teaching a difference on the clothing of the sexes from Deuteronomy 22:5, which many of the old-time commentaries believe is bolstered by I Corinthians 11:1–16, when he said, "It has never promoted a radiant Christian testimony." He hasn't seen some of the youth groups I have seen at our camp and other good, godly camps around America before my blindness. Some of the most radiant testimonies I have ever seen came from modestly dressed feminine girls and ladies! He just hasn't been looking!

Interpreters who only look at one aspect of the meaning of Deuteronomy 22:5 are not being completely honest, just as I would not be honest if I had mentioned only the commandment not to cross-dress and left out the idolatrous practices that we know little about today. Brothers and sisters, be careful lest you handle the Word deceitfully in order to get around this prohibition!

Some modern-day writers may be ignorantly repeating something that others have said or written about this verse. I think some are just parroting what they have been told, but I have read after some men that clearly knew better and made deletions in quotes that led me to believe they didn't want their readers even to know that the other clear meaning existed. Woe to the person that reads and understands the full meaning and conceals part of it for his own purposes!

I will now quote my favorite fundamental Baptist preacher of all time, Dr. John R. Rice. My wife tells me that I actually got to hear this man in my college days, and I know that I have some of his booklets that I read as a young man in high school in the 1960s. He was one of the kindest and yet strongest of conservative, fundamental Bible teachers who ever lived. I now belong to the church he helped build up, Franklin Road Baptist Church in Murfreesboro, Tennessee; and I know the editor of the Sword of the Lord ministries that Dr. Rice started, Dr. Shelton Smith, who is very much like the founder in that he teaches and writes with kindness yet firmness. The passage below is an excerpt from Dr. Rice's book *Here Are More Questions*, which contains many questions that people wrote him and the answers he gave. This particular question is entitled "Women forbidden to wear 'that which pertaineth unto a man'; is it ceremonial law?"

Throughout the first five books in the Bible, the Mosaic law is given. Some of this is moral law, and some of it is ceremonial law. For example, in Exodus 20, the Ten Commandments are given. It is quite obvious that nine of those Commandments are moral law, and these nine are repeated in one way or another in the New Testament. It is just as wrong now to worship idols, to take God's name in vain, to dishonour father and mother, to kill, to commit adultery, to steal, to lie or to covet as it ever was.

But in Colossians 2:14–17 we are plainly told that the Sabbath days given to the Jews and mentioned in the Ten Commandments were nailed to the cross, a part of the ceremonial laws, "a shadow of things to come." But even if one disagrees about the Sabbath question, in the same twentieth chapter of Exodus other ceremonial commands are given, as in verse 24: "An altar of earth thou shalt make unto me, and shalt sacrifice thereon thy burnt-offerings."

So it is wrong to say that any one chapter is all ceremonial and not binding for us—at least it is wrong to say that about Deuteronomy 22. For example, it is clearly a moral problem that a man is not to hide his brother's ox or sheep but must tell where they are. A man must help his neighbor when his ox or sheep is in trouble. Verse 30: "A man shall not take his father's wife, nor discover his father's skirt" is clearly moral law. So chapter 22 does have some moral teachings that are binding upon us today. Of course, no one was ever saved by keeping commandments, but still the moral commandments teach what is right, and Christians want to keep the commandments of God that place moral obligations upon us.

But there is another reason for believing that Deuteronomy 22:5 is a rule that is meant for women of all times. The New Testament clearly teaches that the Old Testament laws about the relations of men and women are still binding. First Corinthians 14:34 says, "Let your women keep silence in the churches: for it is not permitted unto them to speak; but they are commanded to be under obedience, as also saith the law." Here the law means, of course, the first five books of the Bible. So the same doctrine of the Pentateuch is the doctrine of the New Testament when it comes to the relationship of men and women. Women are to be under obedience. Perhaps this refers primarily to Genesis 3:16 where the woman is told, "Thy desire shall be to thy husband, and he shall rule over thee." But certainly the implications that follow are intended also.

In I Timothy 2:11–15 the Scripture plainly says that the Old Testament relationship between men and women is to be the same in the New Testament times.

"Let the woman learn in silence with all subjection. But I suffer not a woman to teach, not to usurp authority over the man, but to be in silence. For Adam was first formed, then Eve. And Adam was not deceived, but the woman being deceived was in the transgression. Notwithstanding she shall be saved in childbearing, if they

The Witness of Your Wardrobe

continue in faith and charity and holiness with sobriety."

In the case of Adam and Eve, the Lord set a certain relationship between husband and wife, and women today are to maintain the same relationship. So we find that this distinction between the men and women was emphasized in the Old Testament by having men and women to dress differently as indications of their different positions. I think it is right to believe that the same distinctions are to be maintained today.

Again, in I Corinthians 11:1–16, the Bible clearly states that in the manner of their hair, women and men are to be different.

"Doth not even nature itself teach you, that, if a man have long hair, it is a shame unto him? But if a woman have long hair, it is a glory to her: for her hair is given her for a covering"—Vss. 14, 15.

And the context plainly says that this difference is based on the fundamental difference in men and women, because "the head of the woman is the man" (vs. 3). You see, Deuteronomy 22:5 is really just a part of the New Testament and Old Testament doctrine of the proper relationship of men and women. And a women should show that she takes a woman's place, should show it by wearing long hair and by wearing woman's clothes. I hope that you will read my book *Bobbed Hair, Bossy Wives and Women Preachers* for further study on this matter.

I think you will see, when you go into the matter thoughtfully, that actually the modern fad of women's wearing slacks and of otherwise defying conventions and trying to be like men is a part of the unchristian rebelliousness of the age. It goes with unbelief and rebellion and not with the most spiritual Christianity. I think lots of good women who mean well have bobbed hair and wear pants and perhaps smoke cigarettes and rebel against their husbands. But they are not as good Christians as they would be if they obeyed the Word of God in this matter, I think. And I think that if they mean well they will come more and more toward the Bible pattern of obedience to husbands and obedience to the conventions which properly differentiate between the sexes and take the place of modest womanhood as taught in the Scriptures and upheld traditionally by the best Christian women. Don't you think so?"

10

OTHER THOUGHTS ON MODESTY

Covering, or Lack Thereof

The Bible refers to clothes as "coverings" for our body (Proverbs 31:22). As I researched clothing, I was touched by how wholesome and pure the ladies from the 1940s and 1950s looked because they were covered. What a time that must have been! (Some of you know that I am legally blind at the time I am writing this and have to use very strong magnifiers to look at or read anything. I grew up in the 1950s but have no memory of it due to complications from having aseptic meningitis in 1995. This project has been an *eye opener* for me!)

Do I think that under a lot of that modest dress were some hypocritical women and societal impropriety that would make some think it was a make-believe world? Of course I know that hypocrisy existed, but it doesn't change the fact that we were all better off in a modest world than we are now in a very immodest secular society! Although some would laugh at me for having this viewpoint, I sincerely believe it.

I have had some Christians literally mock me for the standards we have at our youth camp. Many Christian camps today ignore most, if not all, of the things I say in this book. For instance, I have visited youth camps that

The Witness of Your Wardrobe

have mixed swimming where boys and girls were swimming together in little more clothing than what undergarments would cover. (I didn't go visit the pool area at swim time!) The shorts on the girls as well as the guys showed nearly all the thigh. One *excuse* that was given to me was, "They see more than this in public." That may be true, but that doesn't mean we have to compare ourselves to the public to justify what we are doing. What happened to using the Scriptures for our model?

How the Bible Describes Nakedness

God strongly denounces nakedness in many Scripture passages. (Revelation 3:18; Leviticus, chapters 18–20, and many of the Major Prophets associate nakedness with "shame.") But since the Bible is not a dictionary, we do not have a *definition* of nakedness; however, we do have at least two *descriptions* of nakedness as revealing of thighs. One of these descriptions is found in Isaiah 47:2, 3.

> "Take the millstones, and grind meal: uncover thy locks, make bare the leg, uncover the thigh, pass over the rivers. Thy nakedness shall be uncovered, yea, thy shame shall be seen: I will take vengeance, and I will not meet thee as a man."

Here God condemns nakedness, and we see that one result is no longer being called a "lady"—"thou shalt no more be called, The lady of kingdoms" (verse 5). Is that happening to Christian women today? Are they losing their status of being ladies because of their apparel?

The other description of nakedness as revealing of the thighs is actually found in Exodus 28:42 in reference to the high priest's clothing.

> "And thou shalt make them linen breeches to cover their nakedness; from the loins even unto the thighs they shall reach."

70

This verse lets us know how important the thigh covering is to God. I am not trying to be the ultimate authority on this issue, but these passages make it clear that God's definition of nakedness extends beyond just being unclothed altogether. It also includes wearing clothes that do not cover what they should. Please let us avoid nakedness in any place except within the wonderful confines of the marriage relationship between husband and wife!

Beach Wear

Another interesting book I used for research is entitled *Christian Modesty and the Public Undressing of America.* Jeff Pollard, the author, uses well-documented research to show the effect that public swimming at beaches and pools has had on our society. He has one of the best attitudes of any author I have ever read on this topic. (However, I do disagree with his overall Calvinistic view of theology.) In his book, Mr. Pollard says that the beach has become a place where women feel comfortable unclothing themselves in ways never thought imaginable by early Christians.

Beach volleyball has also taken public undressing to an all-time low. The skimpy, two-piece outfits of the bikini-clad women that play in the Olympics draw attention for more than just their athletic skills. Is this dress appropriate for Christian volleyball teams? I saw pictures from a Christian youth camp where the volleyball players were wearing similar dress to the secular teams, and most of the spectators were male. I wonder why? We must not follow the world's leading in this area!

Some Problems With Uncovering

In *Purifying America,* Alison M. Parker writes a chapter entitled "Mothering the Movies: Women Reformers and Popular Culture," in which she reports on the 1920s and 1930s when Hollywood began to introduce America to a different level of dress and immorality. In fact, it became so bad that the Motion Picture Producers and Distributors of America hired former Postmaster General Will Hays to "oversee upgrading of morals in movies in reaction to continued uprising by citizens for national censorship."

The organization leading the cause to upgrade morals, the WCTU (Women's Christian Temperance Union), believed that they were doing what they had to do for the sake of society, especially the children. The members understood that not all children were being properly guided in their movie attendance; as they said, "We were acting as 'surrogate parents' to help those neglected children who needed to be protected from harmful films."

No wonder great evangelists decried the lack of morals of the "Roaring Twenties"! During this time, women's dresses became shorter (a style that had never been acceptable to any other widely known society), and dancing and drinking became more prevalent. This prompted Christians to lead great movements to save our country. They tried to control some of the damage done by Hollywood, and they successfully voted alcohol out of our country in 1919! To our detriment, the law that banned alcohol was later repealed.

As a result of what Hollywood was showing, American women in the 1920s and 1930s felt pressure to achieve an "ideal" look. In order to achieve that look, they turned to eating disorders. (I thought that was just a modern phenomenon.) *The Social Psychology of Clothing* says that in the eras of the 1920s and the 1960s, the skinny look was the "in" look. It cites a "graph that depicts the average bust-to-waist ratios of models...at four-year intervals during this century....[There was a] decline [in] the 1960s, as well as...around 1925, when busts were deemphasized— the only other time in the century when fashion models have been as noncurvaceous as they are now. It is interesting to note that an epidemic of eating disorders was reported around that time in history, just as such disorders have been prevalent since the 1960s."

It is amazing that a certain look can hold such sway over a society that women will put their lives at risk to fit in! Eating disorders have become such a problem that fashion designers have publicly denounced the ultra-skinny look and refused to allow those models who are severely underweight to be used in certain situations lest they influence teen girls to become anorexic.

We know that only a minority resort to such extremes, but it is clear that society can be greatly influenced by the visual models provided on television and in magazines, Hollywood and other means of mass communication, including the Internet. How much have you been influenced by the fashion industry of the world? We must all be careful to accept the way God made us and realize that our body type is by His design!

God's children should wear designer clothes all the time—clothes that are described by the Designer Himself—God! These clothes were meant to cover our bodies, not reveal them. As you can see, great problems can happen when we don't follow God's plan.

11

SOME SUGGESTIONS FOR US ALL

Let me give you some suggestions based on the principles that I've covered in the book. Please remember that I am making *suggestions,* not *commandments* or *requirements.* I am not trying to make laws or form traditions to uphold biblical principles. I believe in biblical and godly separation but reject all forms of Pharisaism, and I am trying with all my heart to avoid any appearance of legalism—although I really believe legalism has to do with adding to the free gift of salvation. Under no circumstances does dress save a person or keep him saved, but I know some people's definition of legalism is broader, and I seek to avoid that also. I fully expect to be criticized, but I do hope the criticizers will at least try to be reasonable.

I also want you to know that it is not my intention to cast a snare on or be a hindrance to any Christian. Read what Paul says in I Corinthians 7:35:

> *"And this I speak for your own profit; not that I may cast a snare upon you, but for that which is comely, and that ye may attend upon the Lord without distraction."*

The context in which Paul makes this statement is that he is encouraging Christians to remain single if they can do so to better serve the Lord. He is making it clear that

75

this is not a *requirement*, but rather it is a *request* that will help them. It is sad that the Roman Catholics have made this a requirement for many of their church leaders. God didn't want that. First Timothy 4:3 makes that clear.

"Forbidding to marry, and commanding to abstain from meats, which God hath created to be received with thanksgiving of them which believe and know the truth."

This is not an effort to criticize any particular religious group but to prove the point that we can take recommendations from God's Word and make them into laws and traditions God never intended. I do not want to do that.

Some Christians argue that fundamentalists are unloving. Unfortunately, some are unloving, and others may come across as unloving in their remarks. I am sorry for that. However, I would point out that the most unloving things I have ever heard on Christian radio came from famous preachers preaching against Christians like us who are conservative in dress and seek to uphold godliness. They have called us "arrogant," "Pharisaical" and "legalists" that "care more for rules than for people." They say this simply because we disagree with their views of the modesty passages in I Timothy and other places. Where is the love in their words?

Keeping those things in mind, here are my suggestions:

1. Avoid revealing any part of the thigh. This is described as nakedness in the Scriptures.

2. I also recommend that you avoid giving approval for ladies to wear any garment called "shorts." One reason I recommend this is because of the very connotation of the word. Another reason is that our godly Christian fore-fathers strongly denounced the wearing of such garments because they saw them as a compromise. Also, it is very difficult to enforce rules concerning shorts even

when you use words such as "loose fitting" or "walking shorts." I have personally noticed in ministries that I have had the opportunity to observe over a long period of time that shorts have a tendency to get shorter as the years go along. Shorts usually end up showing too much of the hips and figure of the ladies, and there is the added temptation to pull them up ever so slightly, thus revealing the thighs.

Please consider what terms you use when coming up with guidelines for your church and Christian school. Definitions are not all the same. I prefer the term "split skirt" to "culottes," and Modest Apparel USA (www.modestapparelusa.com) sells something called "skorts" that are longer and more feminine than I have ever seen. (I wish some designer would come up with something that I would call "sports skirts." These would be feminine, modest and still allow young ladies to be involved in sports.)

Before you say, "Where are culottes found in the Bible?" I want to remind you that you do not find "shorts" in the Bible or "loose-fitting slacks" either. We are both trying to uphold the same biblical principles in different ways! I am trying to give advice based on biblical principles and observations I have made over the last eight years or so.

I do not know exactly where women's culottes first began to be used publicly. I searched the beginning of the French term and some historical data, but the information was too sketchy for me to say with certainty. It seems that culottes started off in the same strange way as hosiery and stockings. Both supposedly started out as men's garments and were designed differently than they are today. Thankfully, I do not know of any modern-day school that requires men to wear hose, and I hope that day never comes for either hose or culottes! Although we may include some history of trends and the times in our

The Witness of Your Wardrobe

discussion of clothing, we must NEVER lose sight of the principles involved!

I was surprised by something I found folded up in my wife's high school senior yearbook. It was a copy of the local newspaper from Morrisonville, Illinois, dated the year she graduated, 1969. Not only did this newspaper have the local public high school seniors' pictures, but it also had an article addressing the new dress code for the next school year. Here are just some of the guidelines. Please remember that this is from a public school, not a Christian school!

Pants:

1) Boys wearing looped pants must wear a belt.

2) Girls are not to wear slacks, shorts or pants dresses to school or any school-sponsored activity except G.A.A.

Skirts:

Culottes are permitted as long as a panel or flap is in front and back so the garment looks like a dress or skirt. They must be the same length as a dress.

Skirt length:

1) All skirts and dresses must not be over six inches from the floor while kneeling.

2) Under no circumstances should any undergarments be showing.

I want you to know that culottes were recognized and used by public schools. Just because they have grown out of fashion doesn't mean that we can't try to bring them back!

3. I also recommend that you avoid having women wear pants to your church and Christian school functions. This is my reasoning:

a. It is hard to enforce "modest" pants. Again, I have been able to observe many ministries over a long period of time, and those ministries that have gone to pants constantly have to battle with the ever tightening of the pants. I know that their original intention was for women to wear pants that were more feminine and had more "slack" in the slacks, but their decisions about pants are usually influenced by less godly people in their ministries. Eventually, their teen girls end up wearing man-like blue jeans. Where will this lead? What will the pants look like in ten years?

b. Male-looking jeans are the rage, and the advertisements of women wearing these jeans are mostly not appropriate for viewing because they are showing off their figure in lustful ways. If a woman's figure is not enticing, then why do women work so hard at having nice figures to show the public? As Christian ladies, it is okay to work that hard if you're doing it to show your husband. Let us teach our girls that their good figures should be saved for their husbands and that that is a wonderful thing in those confines. On a side note, spandex-type clothing worn under miniskirts is considered acceptable in many Christian circles, but again this is showing off the woman's figure to the public.

c. Even though pant suits are usually worn by older women for the right motives, it is awfully easy to follow trends once the door is open. From what my wife tells me, pant suit outfits are looking more and more masculine. A couple of years ago before I lost my eyesight, I observed this myself when I saw men and women in a restaurant dressed in the exact same suits, ties and all.

4. Shirts or blouses with writing emblazoned across the bosom that would make a boy stop and read carefully should be avoided for obvious reasons. Also, tops that are so tight that underclothing outlines are revealed

should be avoided, also for obvious reasons. When I teach this to young ladies at camp, I hold up pictures of different women dressed differently. Then I ask them if they think that these women are godly. If they say no, I tease them for being a bunch of legalists that judge people based on their clothing. Of course, I am just kidding, but they get the point that all of us, to some extent, form opinions about people based on how they are dressed. Can we all agree on that, at least?

Here is my plea: take what I have written and study it out seriously and with an open heart and mind. Agree with what you can, change something if God so leads you, and do not be critical of others, because we all have to grow and mature at different speeds. Love everybody—hopefully me too! Count me a friend and not an enemy. Be creative in finding ways to incorporate more modesty in your ministries and keep a sweet attitude toward the pastor and school leadership. Give them the benefit of the doubt that they are trying to help, not be "lords over God's heritage" (I Peter 5:3).

I have said this for years: "Nobody can offend me, or at least make me stay offended, by preaching something I do not agree with if I think they are trying to do what is best for others." Will you join me in that? I really do love you, and I write this out of love, not anger.

12

A SPECIAL PLEA TO PASTORS, YOUTH WORKERS AND BIBLE TEACHERS!

Please reconsider the approach that many pastors are taking today: "We won't preach on the subject of dress. We will just model what is right, and the people will catch on." That position seems dangerous to me in such times as these. Dress isn't the only topic I hope you will not be silent about in these days, but it is the topic that I address in this book. I ask you respectfully to reconsider this position of silence for the following reasons:

1. God commands pastors in I Timothy, chapter 2, to address the subject of modest apparel.

> *"In like manner also, that women adorn themselves in modest apparel, with shamefacedness and sobriety; not with broided hair, or gold, or pearls, or costly array. But (which becometh women professing godliness) with good works."—Vss. 9, 10.*

The epistles of I and II Timothy and Titus are often referred to by many as the Pastoral Epistles, because it is generally accepted that they were written to the pastors of the local churches in Ephesus and in Crete to show them and us how to be biblical pastors to our churches. We are not only to teach these things, but we are to do so with the God-given authority suggested in I Timothy 4:11:

"These things command and teach." Notice the word "command." We know that such a command is not based on our authority, but God's.

2. When a pastor does not teach on a subject, he can be robbing his people of an important truth they need to know to make their own intelligent and biblical decisions. Modesty is not the only topic on which I have heard men say they never preach. Most topics that I have heard pastors state they rarely, if ever, address are controversial, including the topic of dress.

I humbly say that we must never let something that is biblical be silent in our pulpits just because it is now controversial. We need to focus more on the fear of God than the fear of man. Let us approach controversial and difficult subjects with compassion and consideration, knowing that many sincere people simply do not know any better; but teach it we must! We may not all agree about what to say, but let us agree to say something because we love God and others.

3. Because we live in a day of compromise and worldly influence, our people need to know what God says about dress and many other difficult topics. Hollywood is destroying many fine Christians by its influence. We must counter this with good, godly, biblical teaching and by taking a public stand in a Christlike manner. Matters such as dating, movie rentals and many issues not mentioned by name in the Bible deserve our attention at appropriate times and places in our churches in order for Christians to have discernment and lead successful Christian lives. I hope this book will give you not only biblical tools, but also some practical and up-to-date information that you can use in any setting.

4. If you use the following rule as a reason for not addressing dress, "Jesus never taught on dress, so nei-

ther do I," be honest with yourself. Do you know what
that leads to?

For instance, do you preach against gambling even
though Jesus never directly addressed that subject? (The
word *gamble* isn't even found in the Bible.) I hope you
do! Do you teach people not to smoke or use tobacco
even though Christ never mentioned tobacco? I hope so.
Do you preach against astrologers predicting our future?
I hope so, but again Christ never directly addressed this.
I could go on and on with things found in other passages
of Scripture but not addressed by Christ that nearly
every concerned pastor addresses for the benefit of his
people. So you can see that this is not a valid reason.

5. Be careful not to let your own experiences (and the
experiences of others you know) determine what you
think on this subject of dress. There is a danger for me
and all of us to be influenced unduly on topics by the
behavior and/or thinking of those around us instead of
the Bible itself. I had a relative of mine get very upset with
me some years ago because I felt so strongly on a controversial topic. I was tempted by my love and respect for
this person just to go along, but I am glad I didn't do it.
Society affects us all. Let us be careful.

6. I believe that society, like never before, needs to hear
from our pulpits on this issue of dress! They need to know
that dress is not just an opinion of the church or a pastoral
preference, but a scriptural principle! The only way godly
ladies will stand up to this world in dress—not only in our
presence, but when we are not present (see Paul's praise
for this in Philippians 2:12)—is to have it settled in their
hearts based on Scripture, not just an opinion.

Some pastors think that as long as their church members model good dress to others they don't need to
preach on it. Don't get me wrong. We must model good
dress, and I think that is one of the best things we can do

on this topic. However, we do not take simply the model approach on gambling and smoking; we address such things from the pulpit also.

7. Pastors, please be consistent! I know pastors who have leadership standards for their staff never mentioned by Jesus or directly by Paul; but if I have a standard that relates to dress, they suddenly attack me, saying, "Jesus didn't teach that!" or "That's not in the Bible!" That is inconsistent.

For example, these pastors will not allow their staff members to smoke. Hopefully, they would try to restore a brother or sister in leadership if they saw him or her smoking; but if that person didn't quit, they would remove them. They do not even mind having a "no smoking" standard for their teachers; but if we have a certain guideline for dress, they call us legalists or unChristlike. That isn't fair!

Do you allow your staff to play the lottery? I hope you don't, for the sake of their testimony and your love for them. Well, I have some guidelines in dress that I want my staff to follow for the same two reasons: their testimony and my love for them.

8. The great evangelists and mightily used preachers of the past addressed the topics of their days that needed to be addressed. Please realize that even though they held and taught high standards of modesty, those highly esteemed preachers were not all a bunch of legalists or completely under their culture's control. They were indeed Bible teachers and sincere preachers of the Word. To suggest they were legalists and blinded by the age in which they lived is ludicrous to many of us.

Disagree with them and us if you must, but please be careful what label you place on others with whom you differ. Immodesty is greatly hurting our Christian brothers, sisters, teens and society as a whole. Please help me try lovingly to help others who struggle in this area! Jesus certainly did address controversial topics. When he dealt with divorce, He was really hitting a hot topic for that day! He did it firmly and gracefully! May we do the same!

For a complete list of available books, write to:
Sword of the Lord Publishers
P. O. Box 1099
Murfreesboro, Tennessee 37133.

(800) 251-4100
(615) 893-6700
FAX (615) 848-6943
www.swordofthelord.com